DENMARK

MAJOR WORLD NATIONS

DENMARK

Alan James

CHELSEA HOUSE PUBLISHERS
Philadelphia

Chelsea House Publishers

Library of Congress Cataloging-in-Publication Data

James, Alan.
Denmark / Alan James.
p. cm. — (Major world nations)
Includes index.
Summary: An introduction to the geography, history, economy,
culture, and people of the smallest and most southerly of the
Scandinavian countries.
ISBN 0-7910-5381-4 (hc.)
1. Denmark—Juvenile literature. [1. Denmark.] I. Title.
II. Series.
DL109.J27 1999
948.9—dc21 99-19238
CIP

ACKNOWLEDGEMENTS

The Author and Publishers are grateful to the following organizations and individuals
for permission to reproduce copyright illustrations in this book:
Cultural Relations Department of the Danish Foreign Ministry; Danish
Dairy Board; the Danish Tourist Board; Photothèque Vautier de Nantxe

CONTENTS

		Page
Map		6
Facts at a Glance		7
History at a Glance		10
Chapter 1	Introducing Denmark	13
Chapter 2	Early Life in Denmark	22
Chapter 3	A Maritime People	28
Chapter 4	Transportation in a Land of Islands	40
Chapter 5	Copenhagen	43
Chapter 6	Other Cities and Towns	51
Chapter 7	The Countryside and Farming	55
Chapter 8	Fishing	61
Chapter 9	Government	65
Chapter 10	Education in Denmark	68
Chapter 11	Danish Traditions	72
Chapter 12	Famous Danes	79
Chapter 13	Living in Denmark	85
Chapter 14	The Economy	92
Chapter 15	Greenland and the Faroe Islands	97
Chapter 16	Denmark in the Modern World	100
Glossary		102
Index		104

FACTS AT A GLANCE

Land and People

Official Name	Kingdom of Denmark
Location	Northern Europe bordering the Baltic and North seas
Area	16,591 square miles (43,000 square kilometers)
Climate	Temperate, humid mild winters and cool summers
Capital	Copenhagen
Other Cities	Arhus, Aalborg, Odense, Nyborg, Randers
Population	5, 333, 617
Major Rivers	Gudenaa
Major Lakes	Lanso
Official Language	Danish
Other Languages	Faroese, Greenlandic, German
Ethnic Groups	Scandinavian, Eskimo, Faroese, German
Religions	Evangelical Lutheran (91 percent)
Literacy Rate	99 percent

Life Expectancy	76.31 years

Economy

Natural Resources	Petroleum, natural gas, fish, salt, limestone, gravel, sand
Division of Labor Force	Private services, 40 percent; government services, 30 percent; manufacturing and mining, 19 percent; construction, 6 percent; agriculture and fishing, 5 percent
Agricultural Products	Grain, potatoes, rape, sugar beets, meats, dairy products
Industries	Food processing, machinery, textiles, electronics, wood products, shipbuilding
Major Imports	Machinery and equipment, petroleum, chemicals, grains, food products
Major Exports	Machinery, meat and meat products, fuels, dairy products, fish, ships, chemicals
Major Trading Partners	Germany, Sweden, United Kingdom, Netherlands
Currency	Danish krone

Government

Form of Government	Constitutional Monarchy
Formal Head of State	King / Queen
Head of Government	Prime minister
Voting Rights	All citizens 18 years of age or older

HISTORY AT A GLANCE

2700 B.C.	In the period called the New Stone Age farmers begin to settle on the land in the area of present-day Denmark. They grow crops and raise farm animals.
4th-11th centuries A.D.	Danish pirates, the Vikings, sail to the coastal areas of Europe and Britain invading and looting. Fierce warriors, they are feared wherever they go.
940-985	The Danish king Harald Bluetooth brings Christianity to his kingdom. He also leads his army to conquer Norway and England.
12th century	Bishop Absalom, a church and secular leader, has the history and folklore of Denmark officially written down. Many beautiful castles and churches are built in Denmark at this time.
1167	The city of Copenhagen is founded around a castle built by Bishop Absalom.
1397	Queen Margrethe unites most of the Scandinavian lands under Danish rule with the treaty called the Union of Kalmar.

14th and 15th centuries	Denmark sees a decline in her powers and has many internal problems partly due to a number of long wars with Sweden.
1530	Lutheran preachers come to Denmark teaching the beliefs of the Protestant Reformation.
18th century	King Frederick IV initiates improvements in education, laws, and the lives of ordinary citizens. Farming and commerce become more efficient and profitable.
1801-1814	Denmark becomes involved in the Napoleonic Wars. All out war ensues after Britain invades Denmark, besieges Copenhagen, and captures the Danish navy.
mid-19th century	Germany attacks Denmark and takes the province of Scheswig-Holstein. Denmark is forced to surrender the area after a treaty in Vienna is signed, causing bitter feelings on the side of the Danes.
1914-1918	Denmark chooses to remain neutral in the First World War but suffers economically due to shortages and embargoes.
1915	Danish women are given the right to vote.
1920	The Treaty of Versailles reverts part of Schleswig back to Denmark. Critical economic conditions plague the country following the world war. Denmark becomes one of the founding members of the League of Nations.

1940   In April German troops invade and force the
               Danish government to give in to their demands.
               Denmark becomes an occupied country of Nazi
               Germany.

1940-1945 The Danes organize a resistance campaign
               against the Germans. They are finally freed from
               German occupation at the end of World War II.

1949   The economy is slow following the end of the
               war. Denmark joins the North Atlantic Treaty
               Organization (NATO).

1950   Archaeologists discover a preserved ancient body
               in the boglands of Denmark. Tollund Man, as it
               is named, is put on display in the Silkeborg
               Museum in Copenhagen.

1953   A new constitution is adopted allowing for a citi-
               zen elected parliament.

1972   Queen Margrethe II succeeds her father,
               Frederick IX, to the throne. She becomes the first
               woman sovereign in Denmark in six centuries.
               Denmark becomes a member of the European
               Economic Community (EEC).

1993   The Maastricht Treaty (Treaty on European
               Union) comes into force. It gives the European
               Union responsibility for decisions on common
               foriegn policy problems and security for all its
               members. It also gives a timetable for the eco-
               nomic and monetary union of Europe. Denmark
               initially rejects the treaty but does eventually sign
               it. Certain points of the treaty continue to be
               debated by the Danish.

1996	Denmark has some internal problems with gang conflicts resulting in a crackdown by Prime Minister Rasmussen. The debate over Denmark's full participation in the European Union (EU) continues.
1999	Work is completed on a bridge and tunnel linking the Danish city of Copenhagen with the Swedish city of Malmö, via an artificial island.
2000	Danish Foreign Minister Niels Helveg Petersen announces resignation. Queen Ingrid dies at ninety years old. Denmark is named the most generous country in helping developing countries, giving a full 1 percent of its GDP.
2001	Copenhagen is named the fourth best city in which to live worldwide by consulting firm William M. Mercer. Former President Bill Clinton makes his first private visit to Europe since leaving office, speaking before Danish business leaders in Copenhagen

1

Introducing Denmark

Denmark is the smallest of the countries of mainland Scandinavia (the others being Norway, Sweden, and Finland). The area of Denmark is 16,600 square miles (43,000 square kilometers). This is about double the size of Wales.

The population of Denmark is 5,333,600. Most of these people live on the islands of Zealand and Funen and on the east coast of Jutland which is sheltered from the North Sea.

Denmark lies at the point where the Baltic Sea joins the North Sea. The only land frontier the country has with Europe consists of 42 miles (about 68 kilometers) of border shared with Germany. But the coastline—or sea frontier—is 5,000 miles (about 8,000 kilometers long). At Elsinore the coast of Sweden is only two and a half miles (four kilometers) away. The coastline and even Swedish buildings can be seen clearly across the water.

Denmark is the most southerly of the Scandinavian countries and in this it is fortunate for the climate is milder than that of those other countries. It is true that very occasionally the channels between some of the islands freeze into solid ice; and cold air from the northeast has been known to reduce the temperature to minus 13 degrees Fahrenheit (minus 25 degrees Celsius) and once, in the hard winter of 1939, to minus 24 degrees Fahrenheit (minus 31 degrees Celsius). But usually in winter Denmark has mild, rainy days and then cold, clear weather. As a maritime country on the edge of the North Sea, Denmark is affected by the presence of so much water. The mild water of the North Atlantic Drift (a current due to prevalent winds) usually raises the temperature in winter above the level that might be expected for a country with such a northerly latitude. Even so, January or February may have average temperatures of 32 degrees Fahrenheit (0 degrees Celsius). July is the warmest month when average temperatures reach 59 degrees Fahrenheit (15 degrees Celsius). On occasions, a heat wave hits the country; the highest temperature recorded in Denmark has been 95 degrees Fahrenheit (35 degrees Celsius).

Annual precipitation (rain, hail, and snow) varies from 32 inches (80 centimeters) in southwest Jutland to 16 inches (40 centimeters) on the islands in the Great Belt (the area of sea between Zealand and Funen). In summer, Denmark may be wet or sunny but there are mild autumns and crops are rarely damaged by early frost. The climate is rather like that of Britain.

Denmark is almost always windy as there are few hills to provide protection from sea breezes from the North Sea and the Baltic Sea. Much of the country is flat. Although in places there are low, rolling hills, Denmark has no real mountains or major rivers. The longest river is the Gudenaa winding through 75 miles

Agricultural land with low, rolling hills. Much of Denmark is flat, and the highest point is only 564 feet (172 meters) above sea level.

(120 kilometers) of Jutland. Few hills are higher than 325 feet (100 meters). The highest point in the country is 564 feet (172 meters), although the hills have names such as Sky Mountain. It is said as something of a joke that most of Denmark is so flat that if you stand on a box you can see the whole country!

The land of Denmark emerged out of the sea about 40 million years ago, and was later submerged by masses of ice on the three occasions when the area was subjected to glaciation and covered with an ice-cap hundreds of meters thick. Huge glaciers came from the north and east and as these enormous currents of ice

15

crossed Denmark (bringing with them rocks and gravel from Norway, Sweden, and Finland) they gouged deep into the subsoil bringing to the surface chalk, sand, and clay. This material was left behind when the ice retreated. In the same way, the hills, valleys, and flat plains of which the country is composed were the work of the glaciers.

The hills in the east of Jutland reach only to 500 feet (150 meters). But a fairly uniform height tells only part of the story, for there are many varied features in the Danish landscape from cultivated lands in the south of Zealand to bare dunes battered by storms on the coast of north Jutland; from heaths and peatbogs in north Jutland to areas of beechwood on the island of Møn, where the trees grow to the clifftops and even in the deep ravines almost down to the sea.

Many Danish towns contain picturesque houses in narrow,

Picturesque houses, such as this one on the island of Funen, can be seen in many towns in Denmark.

An old farmhouse thatched with seaweed—a common sight in Denmark.

twisting streets; and in the countryside there are neat fields and small, whitewashed farmhouses many of which have thatched roofs, in addition to attractive villages and imposing castles.

On the coast there are channels—or small fiords—where the sea has cut into the land. Since the 19th century the people of Denmark have dried out bogs and marshes, and dammed shallow bays and inlets of the sea to enable these areas to be drained. In some cases, the sea water behind dike walls is pumped out, and the area becomes useful arable land where crops can be grown. Nevertheless, part of the Danish coast is still washed away daily by the tide. The Danes try to reclaim this land, in much the same way as this is done in the Netherlands, by erecting land barriers against the encroaching sea. The coastline may move some dis-

17

tance between tides in certain very low-lying, marshy parts of the country. Dunes can be controlled and stabilized—grasses and evergreens are planted to hold the sand, and spruce and fir trees act as windbreaks.

Denmark is a land of green islands. There are about 500 islands altogether of which 100 are inhabited. No one knows exactly how many islands there actually are; some are almost too tiny to be termed islands.

It is useful to identify the various parts of the country and to describe them separately, as these regions differ greatly one from another. If you refer to the map at the beginning of this book, it will help you to understand where the various regions, cities, and towns are located.

The most heavily-populated part of Denmark is not Jutland (the part that projects northward from Germany) but the group of islands—known as an archipelago—further east.

Zealand is the largest island in the archipelago. In medieval times Denmark was a great power in north Europe and the area of her rule included the south of Sweden. At that time, Zealand was situated in the center of the country and not at its eastern end as it is today.

Much of Zealand consists of fairly level clay plains which provide good farming land. The capital city of Denmark—Copenhagen—is situated on the eastern coast of Zealand.

A number of smaller islands lie to the south of Zealand; the important ones are Lolland, Falster, and Møn. These are flat

18

islands rising just above sea level. They have good soil and a mild climate with an early spring and a long summer. Much of Denmark's sugar beet is grown here.

The island of Bornholm stands in a solitary position in the Baltic Sea, 100 miles (160 kilometers) to the east of Zealand. (Because of its separate position it is not included in our map.) Bornholm is a source of the hard rock used for building; cutting granite blocks is an important industry on the island. Bornholm also has fishing villages on the coast and small farms inland. The mild climate allows mulberries and even grapes to grow in the south.

The largest of the western islands of the archipelago is Funen. This island may be considered to have a central position in Denmark's geography. It is often called the "pearl of Denmark" or the "garden of Denmark." It is a beautiful island of small farms and its crops include sugar beet, plums, cherries, hops, and tobacco. The most fertile soil is found in the north of the island. There are many woods on the hills, and heath land on poorer soil.

The south of Funen lies some distance from the busy railway and road in the north which carry passengers across the country from Zealand to Jutland. The south of the island is a more peaceful place where change does not occur very rapidly. The small towns have many houses dating from the 17th and 18th centuries. This is also true of the three main islands to the south of Funen— Langeland, Taasinge, and Aerø.

Jutland (as large in area as the country of Belgium) is the peninsula of land joined to Germany and the largest region of

Good farming land in the north of Zealand.

Denmark—it has 45 percent of the total population. (The area around Copenhagen has 24 percent and the remainder of Denmark 31 percent).

In the east of Jutland there are many small towns and ports on the coast. The climate is mild; this coast is protected from the North Sea by the hills. Although farmers grow barley, oats, wheat, and root crops for cattle on the clay hills, raising dairy cattle and pigs is the most profitable part of the farm income. There are numerous cooperative dairies and bacon factories to process these important products of Danish farms.

The north of Jutland is exposed to the North Sea and consists of flat land battered by gales and sandstorms on the coast. There are high sand dunes along the bleak coastline and large areas of unreclaimed peat bog. There are only a few fishing harbors in the north, such as Skagen and Frederikshavn.

Until 100 years ago there were huge tracts of heath land covering the poor soil of the west of Jutland. Since then, many areas of peat bog and heath have been improved and now comprise important farmlands with fields of potatoes, oats, and rye as well as plantations of coniferous trees.

Western and northern Jutland are thinly populated even though there has been a great deal of land reclaimed from the sea throughout the 20th century.

In the south of Jutland there are meadows and woods. Near the coast there are lagoons and salt marshes.

2

Early Life in Denmark

From the early 19th century, Danish archaeologists have been interested in the human settlement in Denmark in remote times. Over the years, many archaeological finds have been made. These help to paint a clear picture of the lives of the people of long ago.

One of the oldest Scandinavian sites of human settlement was at Bromme in the center of Zealand, where flint tools and bones of reindeer, beaver, and elk were discovered. These belonged to a period about 12,000 years ago. But this period was followed by one of colder temperatures and more limited vegetation during which men may have visited Denmark to hunt reindeer but only during the summer months. Later, when the climate improved again, forests grew up and these gave shelter to bears, wild boar, deer, and primitive cattle. This, in turn, encouraged more hunters. In time, settlers began to migrate to Denmark. These early people lived in small groups and hunted mammals with the aid of tame dogs. They also fished and collected berries to add variety to their diet. They used some flint tools although they mainly used bone to make needles, knives, harpoons, and many other implements, some of which were decorated with patterns of simple figures. Archaeologists sometimes refer to this early period as the Bone Age.

About 7,000 years ago the climate became even milder, and the shape of Denmark changed when water from the melting ice cap caused the land around what is now Denmark to sink under the sea. When the sea broke through to the Baltic, it divided Zealand from the rest of Scandinavia, divided Zealand from Funen, and divided many other land areas from each other. These became small islands. It also divided Britain from Jutland by creating the North Sea. Denmark began to look much as it does today—the peninsula of Jutland protruding north from mainland Europe and, to the east, the large islands of Funen, Zealand, Lolland, and Falster as well as nearly 500 smaller islands.

Bands of settlers arrived in Denmark in increasing numbers. They cleared patches of land by burning the trees and hacking the soil with stone axes fixed to wooden shafts. Then they began to grow crops such as barley and wheat. They also kept sheep, cows, goats, and pigs. Archaeologists have found evidence of houses made of wattle (wickerwork) and daub, and of wood, and round huts in small villages dating from this period of the New Stone Age, beginning in about 2,700 B.C. Farmers led more settled lives than hunters and so Denmark began to be inhabited by people living in permanent communities.

At this time, the large polished flintstone axe was regarded as vitally important—even sacred—for without it these early farmers could not cultivate the forest into farmland. Archaeologists found one axe buried under the floor in a Stone Age dwelling. Its edge pointed upwards and a small bowl had been buried beside it as a gesture to the gods of the earth. The axe meant life to these farmers and death to the trees of the forest.

Later, objects made of bronze and copper were used. Bronze swords, daggers, axe-heads, drinking vessels, and even gold ornaments were obtained from traders from other lands in exchange for furs and for the amber found on Danish beaches. Amber, a gold-colored resin originating from coniferous forests of long ago, was washed up on Danish beaches. Prehistoric women wore amber beads made of this "sea-gold." Increasingly, however, decorative objects were made in Denmark by native craftsmen.

Preserved in the National Museum in Copenhagen are several examples of early clothes found at burial sites. Clothing for a man consisted of a kilt with straps worn over the shoulder, a cloak and a woollen cap; that for a woman included a short skirt of woollen cords, a short-sleeved jacket, and a woollen belt with a large bronze disc as decoration.

From about 2,500 years ago iron began to be used for making weapons and tools. The climate became colder and damper, and more permanent and more comfortable homes had to be built, as protection for both people and farm animals. Clothing became warmer and the people of Denmark began to wear trousers.

About 50 bodies from 2,000 years ago have been found preserved in bog land throughout Denmark. These people may have

Clothing from the Danish Bronze Age, now displayed in the National Museum, Copenhagen.

been thrown into the bogs as sacrifices to the gods (as offerings in the hope that the gods would send crop fertility and good fortune to the people) or perhaps they were killed as a punishment for committing a crime. Some had their throats cut and some, such as the Tollund Man (found in Tollund Bog in Central Jutland in 1950), had been strangled. Some of these early people (women and children as well as men) had been pinned down in the bog by a wooden stake, perhaps as a precaution against them returning to haunt the living. Many of these corpses were found naked and some still had the rope with which they were hanged attached

The Tollund Man, who lived 2,000 years ago and whose body was discovered in a peat bog in Central Jutland in 1950.

around their necks. The stomach contents of the Tollund Man were investigated and this gave archaeologists information about the diet of prehistoric man. He had eaten only a porridge of vegetables and seeds including barley, linseed and the seeds of wild plants. The Tollund Man is displayed in the Silkeborg Museum.

In later years, while Denmark was known to the Romans, they did not penetrate the country as they did many other parts of Europe. Hoards of coins and drinking vessels from Roman times have been discovered in the bogs of Denmark; these show that the north lands had at least some contact with the Romans.

The people who were called Danes had originally lived on

islands off the coast of Denmark or even in Sweden. In time, they seem to have conquered the entire country, and probably the earlier inhabitants who had not been driven away began to intermarry with these conquerors. Eventually, all the inhabitants became known as Danes.

Over the years numerous gold objects have been discovered in Denmark and dated to the fifth and sixth centuries—the so-called Age of Gold. More peaceful, settled conditions of life were found in the seventh century but there were still occasional Danish raids on other lands. Some of the legends of Danish folklore perhaps had their origin in this period, such as that of Harald Bluetooth, a ruler thought to have united the whole country of Denmark and to have died in battle while fighting against the Swedes.

3

A Maritime People

Denmark is almost entirely surrounded by water. It is natural, therefore, that the sea and shipping as well as ports and coastal towns have been important in the history of the islands.

Danish invaders traveled by sea to other countries in Europe from as early as the fourth century until the 11th century. The appearance of Viking ships from Denmark, full of invading pirates carrying swords and axes, struck fear into the inhabitants of the coastal areas of Europe and eastern Britain.

The word *Viking* probably comes from the Old Norse word *vik* (meaning "creek") and seems to mean "men of the creeks"—sea-warriors from the inlets and bays of Scandinavia. Danes, Norwegians, and Swedes all engaged in the profitable business of raiding other countries, for each had bands of sea-roving Vikings who preferred piracy to concentrating on the more humdrum life of cultivating and developing their own land. The Swedes raided the Baltic coasts and the Danes and Norwegians looted Britain and the French coast. Some Vikings traveled round the coast of

Spain into the Mediterranean; others went to the Faroe Islands, Iceland, and Greenland.

The pirates from Denmark found France easy prey and even England was fairly simple to reach by ship, despite the long and arduous voyage across the North Sea. The first successful raid on England in 793 (when Lindisfarne Abbey on Holy Island was looted and burned) was followed by others; and also by raids on Scotland, Wales, and Ireland.

The Vikings soon realized that raiding the coastal regions of other countries involved them in little danger. Fleets of Viking ships would appear unexpectedly off the coast and, before the

A reconstruction of a Viking ship, used by tourists but reminiscent of those used by the fierce warriors of bygone days.

local inhabitants had time to do anything sensible or even managed to protect themselves, the invaders would be ashore, destroying, murdering, and carrying off treasure, booty, and slaves to their ships. Then they would sail away before help and reinforcements could arrive from places further inland.

The Viking ships were the finest in Europe—light, fast, strong, and seaworthy. The prow and stern were almost identical. The ships were steered by a large oar, and although most had a square sail, they also had a bank of oars. The remains of Viking ships from Denmark which have been found are mainly of oak.

Traces of the Danish occupation of the north and east of England survive in the names of over 2,000 towns and villages which are of Scandinavian origin, such as places with names ending in *toft* (meaning "homestead"), *thorpe* (meaning "hamlet"), *beck* (meaning "stream"), *by* (meaning "town"), and *wick* (meaning "creek").

Various kings of Denmark were so powerful and well-organized that they were able to command in excess of 1,000 troop ships. The remains of Viking barracks have been discovered in different parts of Denmark. These barracks were, in effect, castles with surrounding ramparts. The barracks at Trelleborg on Zealand, for

The Jelling Stone, which bears the runic inscription: "King Harald caused these mounds to be raised to Gorm his father and to Tyra his mother; the Harald who won for himself all Denmark and Norway and made the Danes Christians."

example, had a layout that called for military precision. Such barracks, showing a detailed military organization in Denmark, help to explain the success of the Danish raids abroad.

At the end of the ninth century, the English king, Alfred the Great, built a fleet and began to attack the Viking ships out at sea before they had a chance to reach the English coast.

Gorm the Old was the first king to unite the whole of Denmark (Jutland and the islands) into one land. About this time, the people of Scandinavia evolved a form of writing in runic characters which represented the sounds in their language. These runes were wedged-shaped, composed of straight lines and angles, so that they were easy to carve on wood, stone, bone, or metal. Names of people were inscribed on weapons and jewelry to make them powerful. Runes were also written on gravestones in memory of those who had died. One example of this is the large Jelling Stone erected in about 980 A.D. by King Harald Bluetooth in memory of his father, Gorm the Old, and his mother, Tyra. (The present royal family of Denmark is able to trace its descent back to Gorm the Old in the tenth century). Runes probably began to be used in Denmark in about 100 A.D. It seems that inscriptions and pictures were cut on stone and then colored by painting in order to bring out their beauty more fully.

Gorm the Old had an even more famous great-grandson called Canute. He became king of England, Denmark, Norway, and even of southern Sweden. When the Danes arrived in England they made camps at the estuaries of rivers and from there took

32

An equestrian statue of Bishop Absalon in Copenhagen.

control of large areas of land. At times, instead of destroying everything they found, they agreed to accept ransom (called *Danegeld*) from the native population. Some of them even became settlers, learning the local language, accepting local customs, and marrying into the native population. Some also agreed to be baptized as Christians; but, since they did not wish to offend the Scandinavian gods Odin and Thor, it is thought that they washed the baptismal sign of the cross out of their hair before returning to their native land. Yet this "Danish Empire" in Europe was short-lived—Denmark lost England soon after Canute's death.

The people of Denmark also went to war with the Estonians who lived on the eastern shores of the Baltic Sea and with the

33

Wends—Slavonic people living on the south shore of the Baltic. These battles continued as late as the 13th and 14th centuries.

Two important Danish leaders in the 12th century were King Valdemar the Great and Bishop Absalon. They built a number of fine castles and churches. Absalon had seen that other European countries had details of their past recorded in chronicles and he decided that Denmark, too, as a growing nation state, ought to have a detailed history of her land. So he gave one of his clerks, named Saxo, the task of producing a history of Denmark. This included old myths and sagas of folklore from ancient times as well as an historical account of the lives and exploits of Danish kings and nobles.

Now the first Danish laws began to be written down. In time, the different laws of the various regions and settlements throughout Denmark became unified for all parts of the country.

One tradition dating from this period of Danish history is of the origin of the flag of Denmark (a white cross on a red background). In 1219, the Danes were losing a battle in Estonia when a flag suddenly fluttered from the sky. The Danes, according to the legend, accepted the flag as their own, took courage, and won the battle. The flag of Denmark is the oldest flag of any European nation. It is called the *Dannebrog* in Danish—meaning a piece of red cloth.

At the end of the 14th century, Queen Margrethe, the first woman to govern Denmark, united most of Scandinavia under one crown by the Union of Kalmar (1397). This was designed to ensure peace in Scandinavia, with the three kingdoms of

Denmark, Norway, and Sweden united under one monarch. Under Queen Margrethe, Denmark became the most powerful nation in the Baltic. Sweden left the union shortly afterwards but Norway and Denmark remained united until 1814.

There were often internal troubles in Denmark in the 14th and 15th centuries. Even the alliance with Norway was uneasy at times, for Denmark always played the role of the dominant power. For several hundred years the power of Denmark declined, partly because a number of long wars with Sweden drained the resources of the country. But in the 18th century, King Frederick IV improved education, the law, and the welfare of the ordinary citizens. In addition, later in the century, farming and commerce also became more efficient.

An important and lucrative source of revenue for the state of Denmark for a number of centuries was money paid to allow ships to pass through the Sound (strait) going to or from the Baltic Sea. These dues were collected by the Danes from ships as they passed Elsinore (the scene of William Shakespeare's play, *Hamlet*). Kronborg Castle guards the sound at Elsinore. The payment of these "Sound Dues" remained a controversial issue for centuries, although the Danes argued that Denmark had to maintain a complex system of lighthouses among the 500 islands and shallow channels for the benefit of international shipping and that other nations should pay for the service.

During the Napoleonic Wars, Denmark attempted to remain aloof from the main conflict in Europe and joined the League of

Kronborg Castle, which guards the Sound at Elsinore.

Armed Neutrality, with Sweden and Russia. But a British fleet, when refused permission to pass Kronborg Castle and enter the Baltic, bombarded Copenhagen. In 1801, the British navy, under Admiral Lord Nelson, won the Battle of Copenhagen. It was at this battle that Nelson, placing a telescope to his blind eye when Admiral Parker was signaling him to retreat, continued fighting until victory was certain. Six years later, in 1807, Britain demanded that Denmark should give up her navy (so that it could not be used by Napoleon against the British navy during the war). When the Danes refused this demand, a British force landed in Denmark and besieged Copenhagen which was forced to surrender within three days. The British force was led by Sir Arthur Wellesley (later to become the Duke of Wellington) and his horse

36

was named "Copenhagen" to commemorate the occasion. The British took away most of the Danish fleet; and from then until 1814 Denmark and Britain were at open war, with Denmark quickly building small craft, engaging in gunboat war, and inflicting much damage on British shipping.

In 1814, Denmark lost Norway, which had been eager to free itself from Denmark but which then became involved in a further union, this time with Sweden.

In the mid-19th century Denmark was attacked by Germany and had to give up the province of Schleswig-Holstein in the south. The conflict between the two countries was finally settled by the Treaty of Versailles. Then the northern part of Schleswig was returned to Denmark in 1920, as a result of the free choice of the people who lived in that region; while the southern part voted to remain within Germany.

When the First World War began in 1914, Denmark was in a vulnerable position at the entrance to the Baltic Sea. It decided to close off its waters since Germany had threatened to lay mines in them. Denmark was a neutral country during the war—meaning that it did not actively support either side. It traded with the fighting nations and earned a great deal of money, although about 100 of its ships were torpedoed as a result of German submarine action.

It was during the war, in 1915, that Danish women were given the right to vote alongside men.

In the period between the two world wars, the Danish economy went through a crisis because industrial production and commerce had been geared to meeting the demands of the First World

War. The inter-war period was a time of change and innovation in Denmark. Then came the Second World War.

On a sunny morning in April 1940, German troops marched north into Denmark. German ships entered the harbor at Copenhagen and German bombers flew over the city. The Danish government was forced to give in to German demands and the country became an occupied land. As the war progressed, Denmark found the German occupation increasingly irksome and hard to bear. Many of the Danish people drew courage from the example of their king, Christian X, who continued to ride his horse through the streets of Copenhagen, despite occasional outbursts of gunfire. The king went out alone and unprotected, and the Danes raised their hats to their monarch as he calmly rode through the streets of the capital.

The Danes now began to organize an effective resistance cam-

King Christian X, riding through the streets of Copenhagen on his 72nd birthday in 1942. His courage during the German occupation was a source of inspiration to the Danish people.

paign to make things difficult for the occupying foreign troops. The Danish resistance fighters developed into sabotage groups. By 1943 there were disturbances and strikes in a number of Danish towns. And a Freedom Council was formed in order to direct the efforts of the resistance groups. Groups of youths even put sugar into the gasoline tanks of the invaders' vehicles and slashed their tires.

An old six-story building in Copenhagen was used as Gestapo (German Secret Police) Headquarters in Denmark. The attic at the top of the building was used as a prison for those Danes who were being held as suspected resistance fighters. Elsewhere in the building there were offices containing files on many individual Danes. So the Danish resistance movement asked the British Royal Air Force (R.A.F.) to bomb the building. It was bombed from a low level by 18 British planes which aimed the bombs into the lower floors of the building to avoid killing the Danish prisoners held in the attic. The R.A.F. raid was a success, the Gestapo records were destroyed in the wreckage, and most of the prisoners managed to escape from the attic in the resulting confusion. But the raid had a tragic result, too, for a school was hit by accident and 80 children died.

The facts of history are seldom simple to explain. The occupation of Denmark was a complex affair which lasted until the war ended in 1945. Then Denmark was again a free land.

The Danes made a rapid recovery, in both political and economic organization. Denmark is now one of the most advanced countries of Europe, with a high standard of living.

4

Transportation in a Land of Islands

Most of the major cities and towns of Denmark are situated on the coast because of the importance of the sea, shipping, and communications between one island and another. Because every part of Denmark is close to the sea, the Danes have had to develop an efficient system of getting from one island to another with the minimum of fuss. There are numerous ferry services for passengers, vehicles, and trains; and also many vessels carrying cargo. In addition, there are countless yachtsmen who enjoy boating more as a hobby than a necessity.

From Copenhagen there is a hydrofoil service which crosses the Sound to Malmö in Sweden.

There are many fine, modern roads in Denmark—most of them built in fairly straight lines—and a large number of bridges. The island of Falster is joined to Zealand by the Great Stream Bridge, which is about two miles (three kilometers) long—and one of the longest bridges in Europe. Falster is joined to the nearby island of

An aerial view, showing the bridges which span the Little Belt, the channel of water which separates Funen from Jutland.

Lolland by yet another bridge, so making travel and communication relatively easy in this land of islands.

A busy road and a railway run across Zealand from Copenhagen. Vehicles and trains then board a ferry at Korsør for the trip of 50 minutes across the Great Belt to the port of Nyborg on the island of Funen. The route crosses Funen and then there are two bridges over the channel of water called the Little Belt (separating the island of Funen from Jutland). The route then continues across Jutland to Esbjerg on the North Sea coast. The distance between Copenhagen and Esbjerg is 175 miles (280

41

kilometers) but the system of transportation is so efficient for motor vehicles and trains, and ferries are so frequent, that traveling from one place to another is effected fairly quickly.

Very many Danes own bicycles and there are bicycle paths alongside some roads to allow cyclists to travel in safety. There is parking allotted for bicycles as well as cars, and some buses have hooks at the back where bicycles can be placed when their owners board the bus for a long journey. There are long-distance bus services on the Zealand to North Jutland ferry route, and local bus services operate from all towns.

Denmark does not manufacture automobiles; most of those on the roads are imported from Japan, Britain, and Germany. In addition to all the bicycles on the Danish roads (many of which carry small children on passenger-seats at the back), some Danes also ride motorcycles.

The Danish State Railways runs efficient and comfortable rail services to all parts of Denmark. Where a train journey involves crossing the Great Belt it is necessary to transfer to a ferry, although express trains go right onto the ferry, and passengers may leave their luggage on the train and have a meal in the ferry restaurant.

For those who prefer air travel, the airport at Copenhagen has regular flights to a number of towns in Jutland such as Esbjerg, Odense on Funen, and Rønne on the island of Bornholm.

There are also many international flights from Copenhagen including intercontinental flights to and from the United States and Canada, the Far East, and Africa.

5

Copenhagen

The city of Copenhagen was founded in the year 1167 when Bishop Absalon built a castle on the site of what is now Christiansborg Palace—part of which is the present parliament building. Yet much of the old town of Copenhagen was destroyed by fires in the 18th century or bombardment by the British at the time of the Napoleanic Wars. A large part of the city is therefore relatively new, with wide, well-planned avenues and tree-lined streets.

Copenhagen has been the most important city in Denmark since the 15th century. The capital of Denmark was once Roskilde to the west of Copenhagen but in the 15th century King Erik moved to Copenhagen and the city became the military, commercial, and cultural capital of the country. The old capital, Roskilde, is the place where virtually every Danish king and queen has been buried for the past 500 years.

In the 17th century, King Christian IV doubled the size of Copenhagen, erecting the Rosenborg Palace and other magnificent buildings and laying out a greatly extended capital.

The royal tombs in Roskilde Cathedral. Almost every Danish king and queen for the past five hundred years has been buried here.

Copenhagen is now both a busy capital city and a friendly, quaint place; everywhere the old and historic city blends with the new and modern city. Its Danish name is *København* which means "Merchants Harbor."

Copenhagen is also the site of the residence of the royal family at Amalienborg Palace. Each day when the monarch is in residence the ceremony of the changing of the guard takes place outside the palace. The soldiers wear blue uniforms (or red ones on the monarch's birthday) with high bearskin hats and they carry swords.

The University of Copenhagen was founded in the 15th century. The Copenhagen Rådhus (or City Hall) is an imposing red brick building; the City Hall Square forms the busy and important center of Copenhagen. The city has a skyline of copper steeples, spires, and towers. (There is also a marble church with a large copper dome.) Copenhagen is sometimes referred to as "the city of beautiful spires."

There are more than 70 museums and art galleries in the capital as well as Rosenborg Palace in which the Crown Jewels are kept. The National Museum contains one of the most comprehensive collections of Stone Age artifacts in the world. Another museum shows how the country has developed since the very earliest period. In the New Carlsberg Sculpture Gallery the con-

The Rådhus, or City Hall, in the center of Copenhagen.

tents range from Greek, Roman, and Egyptian sculptures to modern Danish sculptures. One of the statues in the garden outside the museum is Rodin's *The Thinker*.

The city also has a Royal Arsenal and Military Museum, a Stock Exchange building (dating from the 17th century, with a spire of four twisted dragons), and a museum dedicated to the works of Denmark's most famous sculptor, the 18th-century Bertel Thorvaldsen.

In the center of the city is the Tivoli pleasure garden which dates from 1843 and which is open each year from the spring until the autumn. There are boating lakes and flower gardens, foun-

A young drummer in the Tivoli Boy Guards—his uniform is very similar to that of the monarch's guard outside Amalienborg Palace.

The Little Mermaid, Copenhagen's special symbol, perched on a rock at the entrance to the harbor.

tains, theaters, a fairground (from the top of the Big Wheel you can see the whole city spread out below), and bandstands. The Tivoli Boy Guards, dressed in uniforms that are replicas of those of the monarch's guards, parade through the grounds and look like toy soldiers. At night, the gardens are illuminated with thousands of colored lights. Impressive displays of fireworks are staged at weekends and holidays.

The shopping center of Copenhagen, called *Strøget,* is a pedestrian precinct of five streets, one following another in a winding line from City Hall Square to King's New Square. Shoppers may wander here without fear of traffic. The commercial area of the city is beside King's New Square.

Alongside the harbor is the Langelinie, a coastal road from which can be seen *The Little Mermaid*, the bronze statue by Edvard Eriksen (he used his wife as the model). This has long been the special symbol of Copenhagen. The little figure of the mermaid perched on a rock gazes out across the harbor.

The New Harbor (which has had this name since the 17th century) is a canal bordered by brightly-painted old houses and night-clubs and tattoo shops often frequented by visiting sailors.

The Royal Copenhagen Porcelain factory is where plates, jugs, bowls, vases, and figures of high quality are made, and where expert artists paint the objects that have been fired in kilns. The trademark of the factory is three wavy blue lines representing the Danish waterways—the Sound, the Great Belt, and the Little Belt.

There is also a Permanent Exhibition of Danish Arts and Crafts in Copenhagen. Articles from this exhibition—porcelain, glass, silver, wood, and so on, including Danish toys—are for sale.

Copenhagen is a busy capital city and more than one quarter of the Danish population lives in the city or in the suburbs surrounding it. There are theaters there (including Copenhagen's main theater, the Royal Theater), the Royal Danish Ballet, cinemas, and restaurants. There are parks and canals and, at the docks, there is a constant bustle from the ships of many nations berthed at the quays to be loaded or unloaded—for the city is the most important port in Scandinavia. The quays are so large that 350 ships can berth at once, and there is almost no tide to cause

The New Harbor in Copenhagen—note the brightly-painted houses alongside the canal.

difficulties for the arrival and departure of ships. There are also busy shipyards where new ships are built. There is the taste of salt in the air from the sea, and seagulls as well as pigeons wander the city squares. Huge ships seem to be just at the ends of busy streets filled with traffic.

Not all parts of Copenhagen are situated on Zealand. Part of the capital is on the island of Amager; so the capital is built on two separate islands. The strait of water between is a natural harbor and provides shelter for ships. The part of Copenhagen built on the island of Amager has attractive canals and old houses (that once belonged to prosperous merchants and traders), modern offices, and blocks of apartments–a mixture of the old and the

49

new. Drawbridges cross the strait to the rest of Copenhagen; and these drawbridges need to be raised to allow ships to pass.

Copenhagen is the main manufacturing city in Denmark and, apart from the construction of engineering goods such as marine engines and electrical apparatus, there are flour mills, oil-seed crushing factories, breweries, and a margarine factory. About half the industry and commerce of the country are carried on in the capital, and yet Copenhagen is an attractive city.

It is also a colorful city with postmen in scarlet coats, and soldiers in blue uniforms; red sentry boxes; green and gold turrets, domes and spires; the sparkle of the changing blue of the sea; and, just outside the city, green fields and woods.

Flora Danica porcelain, one of the most famous products of the Royal Copenhagen Porcelain factory. The silverware shown here is from the Georg Jensen factory.

6

Other Cities and Towns

Aarhus (also spelled Arhus), situated on the east coast of Jutland, is the next largest city after Copenhagen. The area around Aarhus is the most densely populated part of the Jutland peninsula. Aarhus is an important port (importing coal and fertilizers and exporting much of the dairy produce of Jutland) and has busy docks where ships are built and repaired, as well as industries such as textiles, margarine, beer, and refrigerators.

Aarhus has a red brick cathedral with a green copper roof. The city also has an open-air museum where there are townhouses from various parts of Jutland that have been re-erected on a single site to form a reconstructed old town. This is very picturesque with cobbled streets, and a stream running through it.

Aarhus has splendid beaches, hotels and restaurants and many visitors spend their holidays in the city where there are narrow, winding streets near the harbor.

There are parks and Botanical Gardens, nature trails and a sporting complex. One of the bodies discovered in the peat bog long ago can be seen in the museum. The University of Aarhus dates from the early 20th century.

Odense is the third largest city in Denmark and an important center of engineering and shipbuilding. It is situated in central Funen but joined to the sea by a canal five miles (eight kilometers) long; and so it is a bustling port even though its situation is inland. Small ships travel up the canal carrying fuel, fertilizers, and manufactured goods to the people of this agricultural island.

The city has a modern town hall. In contrast, the oldest building in the city is the brick-built cathedral which dates from the 13th century. One garden in the city is a memorial to Hans Christian Andersen, the story writer who was born in Odense and whose birthplace is now a museum containing his personal possessions as well as copies of his books translated into many languages.

Hans Christian Andersen's birthplace in Odense, now a museum.

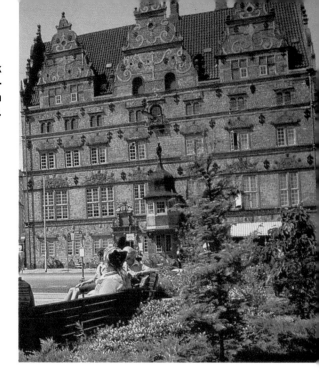

Jens Bang's Brick House, a six-story building from the early 17th century.

Aalborg (in the north of Jutland) is the fourth largest city in the country and, like the others, it has a port and shipbuilding yards and such industries as beer, cement, fertilizers, tobacco, and the Danish drink *schnapps*. The clay of north Jutland is used in the brick-making industry. The chalk is used to make cement.

The central part of this attractive city is a traffic-free area. The museum contains relics of the Viking age. Jens Bang's Brick House is a six-story building surviving from the early 17th century. At that time bricks were unusual and expensive. These old brick buildings in Denmark were made with red bricks manufactured from surface clay. More modern brick buildings have yellow

53

bricks which have been produced from clay that has had to be extracted from the ground.

Aarhus, Odense, and Aalborg are large cities but all three are only a fraction of the size of Copenhagen. Similarly, the towns of Denmark, although important in themselves, are perhaps even less than half the size of the cities. Two of these towns are Esbjerg and Randers.

Esbjerg, on the North Sea coast of Jutland, began to grow into an important town after the railway line was built across Jutland in 1874. Much of the town was built towards the end of the 19th century. The port of Esbjerg receives visitors arriving by ship for holidays in Denmark and is also an important port for the export of farm produce.

Esbjerg has two other points of special interest: a sea-water aquarium and an art gallery devoted to works of modern art.

Randers, lying to the north of Aarhus in Jutland, is typical in having a long history. Like other Danish towns, Randers has a variety of factories which produce a range of commodities, including bacon which is packaged for export.

7

The Countryside and Farming

Until the latter part of the 19th century, Denmark was a poor agricultural country, growing mainly wheat and exporting the grain to other European countries. But then the competition from the wheat fields of the United States (where grain could be grown more cheaply) meant that Denmark lost many of its former markets; and for a period the country was in financial difficulty. Since that time Denmark has gone through important agricultural changes that have influenced its farming. Apart from using new fertilizers, and new machinery (milking machines, tractors, and harvesting equipment) to make jobs on the farm easier and quicker, and draining the land (using clay pipes which help the soil to dry out quickly after winter), farmers began to keep pigs, chickens, and dairy cows. Thus they started to sell butter, bacon, eggs, cheese, and condensed milk to other countries. And so cows, pigs, and chickens saved the economy of the country. The prices obtained for bacon and butter in the markets of western Europe

Red Danish dairy cows, the most widespread breed in the country.

rose steadily. The Danes saw an opportunity to channel their agricultural energies into dairy farming.

About 60 percent of the land of Denmark is now used for agriculture. The Danes have worked hard to make each plot of cultivated land produce as much as possible. Most farms are small and are owned by the families who work the land. Denmark's economic health is still partly dependent on farming, even though only five percent of the population now works on the land.

Cooperative societies began to thrive in Denmark in the 1880s when each farmer in a particular area contributed a share of the money needed to set one up. A cooperative can afford to build a large dairy to make butter from the milk produced daily on each small farm. A cooperative can also do what a small farmer with limited resources could never do. In addition, it lends money to farmers to improve their farms. Some cooperatives build bacon factories. Although some farmers sell their produce to commercial

56

firms, many farmers deal directly with a cooperative. The bulk of the export trade of such produce, for example, is handled by the farmers' cooperatives. Through efficient marketing the cooperatives have been able to obtain higher prices for high-quality produce. Some cooperatives even purchase cattle food, fertilizers, cement, and coal.

Red Danish cows (actually a reddish-brown) and Jutland cows (black and white) supply rich milk for the dairy industry. Many cows in Denmark used to be milked three times a day. Most farmers now only have the time to milk twice a day.

Cream is removed from the milk and made into butter. Some of the skimmed milk that remains when the cream is removed is returned to the farms for feeding the pigs. The butter is churned in stainless steel churns, packed in foil, and much of it is exported. In order to make cheese, the milk is made to go sour. The whey is drawn off and the remaining curd is turned into cheese. Danish blue cheese is famous but there are many other Danish cheeses. The Danes enjoy eating cheese, even for breakfast.

There are more pigs in Denmark than there are Danes. When pigs have grown to the required weight, they are killed for bacon. The bacon joints are "cured" in a bath of brine (salt water) for four days. The bacon is branded *DANMARK: DANISH*. Other pigs are used to make luncheon meat and sausages.

Many farms in Denmark have large arable fields without hedges where barley, wheat, rye, oats, grass, clover, beets, and potatoes are grown. But on most farms dairy cattle and pigs are the most profitable part of the farm economy. The islands of

Blue-veining Danish blue cheese.

Denmark produce a wide range of crops and have a high output due to the mild climate. On the poorer, sandy soils of central, north, and west Jutland, grains and potatoes give a lower yield. Barley is grown to feed the pigs, and some sugar beet is fed to the cows; but there is also much grass for summer grazing. Grain is grown on 60 percent of the cultivated land of Denmark; root crops on 10 percent; grass or green fodder on 25 percent; and the remaining five percent is devoted to seed production.

There are thousands of market gardens in Denmark, especially on Zealand and Funen. Danish horticulture covers the production of fruit in orchards, vegetables, flowers, tobacco, and hops. Produce ranges from Danish apples to morello cherries which are used to make brandy. Many ordinary farms also have orchards of fruit trees. One unusual kind of farm found in Denmark is the mink farm. The Scandinavian countries produce much of the world's mink and Denmark is one of the major producers. In Copenhagen there are some world-famous fur houses which sell mink coats.

Forests cover only about one-tenth of Denmark and many small copses of beech, lime, elm, and oak have been planted. Denmark is part of the lightly-forested area of northern Europe, although the country has fine beech woods—some of which practically border the city of Copenhagen.

The farms of Denmark are a model to the world. They show

Although Denmark is only lightly-forested, there are many fine beech woods such as this. The beech is the national tree of Denmark.

how a country can alter and expand its system of agricultural production to meet the needs of changing markets. But it remains to be seen for how long the present prosperous situation will continue. Demand for the products of Danish farms has not increased as rapidly as the supply. The Danes have to face competition from dairy producers in other countries. People in Europe are becoming increasingly conscious that butter, cream, and animal fats are associated with coronary heart disease and some have decided to eat less of these products. Many farmers living near Copenhagen have sold their cows and find it more profitable to grow fruit, flowers, and vegetables for sale in and around the capital.

In recent years, the Danes have been so successful in farming that other countries have copied their methods. The result was that they were faced with so much competition that they were forced to diversify (that is, to devote their energies to a number of different aspects of farming). Danish eggs, for instance, used to be sold in many European countries. Poultry farmers in other countries then improved their own methods of keeping chickens in batteries, copying the Danes, and the demand for Danish eggs lessened.

It is likely that Danish farmers will be forced to diversify again and again in order to produce what is currently in greatest demand in the markets of Europe and the world.

8

Fishing

No place in Denmark is situated more than about 30 miles (about 50 kilometers) from the sea. Denmark has almost 300 ports. Much cargo is sent from one part of the country to another by sea and, similarly, many people travel from place to place by boat. Thousands of Danes earn their livelihood by fishing from the large fleet of motor vessels. As a result Denmark also has an industry which provides trawlers, nets, refrigeration equipment,

Fishing boats in one of Denmark's many harbors.

Danish fishermen working at sea. Fishing is one of Denmark's major industries and a source of livelihood for thousands of Danes.

and processing, as well as packing and distribution facilities. The fishermen of Denmark have larger catches than those of any other country in the European Union.

The main fishing harbors and fish-processing centers in Denmark are located along distinct sections of the coastline. The most important fishing harbors are in the west of the country on the Jutland peninsula—from Frederikshavn in the northeast down to Esbjerg. The port of Esbjerg has deep-water berths for ships. A fleet of over 500 fishing boats is based there. But most coastal villages in all parts of Denmark have a few small boats engaged in fishing, either out at sea or in the belts and sounds (the waters between the islands).

The waters between Denmark and Norway (the Skagerrak) and

Denmark and Sweden (the Kattegat) are commonly fished, as is the Baltic Sea. But a major source of Denmark's fish is the North Sea. The sea around Denmark contains cod, mackerel, flatfish, shrimps, and herring; while halibut and plaice are caught on the fishing banks in the North Sea. Sand eel, Norwegian pout, and sprat are caught as "industrial" fish—used to make fishmeal, oil, and stockfood.

At the Fish Market in Copenhagen, fishermen's wives serve customers with fish from boxes, right at the edge of the sea. There are also juicy shrimps and oysters. At fresh fish shops the fish are kept alive in tanks until bought. Indeed, customers may point out the very fish they would like.

The Danish island of Bornholm in the Baltic Sea is well-known for herring. The fish are cleaned and hung to dry in the open on wooden bars. Then they are placed in the smokehouse where they are smoked over wood fires. Many smoked herring are exported.

The small wooden Danish fishing boats are often crewed by four or five men from the same locality who may have known one another for years; or perhaps by a family—a father passing his skills and knowledge on to his sons. The boats have equipment such as echo-sounders and short-wave radio.

Most fishing is done using seine nets and floating trawls. The boats that journey to the fishing grounds in the North Sea take stocks of ice to keep the fish fresh on the journey back. The boat may be at sea for as short a time as ten days or as long as 30 days, so the crew must take sufficient food to last them for a long trip. Some travel 200 miles (320 kilometers) from Denmark and,

Smoked herring, popular in Denmark and abroad.

unless bad weather stops them, they will continue to fish until they have a really good catch.

Most fish are sold at auction markets in Denmark although some catches from the North Sea are taken straight to Britain. Denmarks railway is system is an advantage in getting fish quickly from port to customers in Europe.

Most of the fish goes to a local factory close to the fishing port as soon as they have been auctioned. Fish are filleted and frozen fresh or perhaps smoked or canned and then sold in Denmark itself or for export.

Government

Each parish and tiny village in Denmark contributed one stone to be placed in the granite walls of Christiansborg, the building in which the parliament meets. This signified that parliament has a real and lively contact with the people, the affairs and the problems of the entire nation.

Royal power was limited in Denmark in 1849 when the first parliamentary constitution was introduced. In that year King Frederick VII agreed to a demand from the people that he should give up his absolute power. The new constitution was signed by the king on June 5, 1849. This gave Denmark its first democratic government elected by the people. This date in June is still celebrated as the National Day in Denmark.

The Act of Succession, which decides who the next Danish monarch will be, was amended in 1953 to allow Princess Margrethe to succeed to the throne. She became the first queen to rule the country since the 14th century. Previously, women had not been allowed to succeed to the throne and it is typical of

The Danish Parliament in session—note the push-button system of voting.

Danish commonsense that the Danes merely decided to change the rules!

Government in Denmark is by means of a single-chamber parliamentary system with a constitutional monarchy, as in Norway and Sweden. The king or queen of Denmark is head of state and appoints and dismisses the prime minister and other cabinet ministers. The aim of government is to promote a stable and secure democracy in which all adults have the right to vote in elections for the parliamentary representatives of their choice.

The government (both at national and local levels) provides postal and transportation services, and operates telephones, electricity, gas, ports, and road construction through concession companies. The government does not directly become involved in industrial or agricultural production.

The members of parliament are elected at the general election every four years. They are elected by a system of proportional representation. This makes sure that each political party has a number of members of parliament related to the actual number of votes cast by the people for that particular party.

There are several political parties in Denmark. The Social Democrats usually hold more seats than any other party in parliament. The next largest parties are the Conservatives, the Socialist People's Party, the Liberals, and the Center Democrats. Parliament always includes two members from the Faroe Islands and two from Greenland, as these islands are part of the kingdom of Denmark.

Each political party works for security, justice, and happiness for the people of Denmark. As in all countries, the parties may disagree on the precise methods of achieving these aims—whether, for instance, the government should take an important lead in economic life or leave much scope to private enterprise. This multiparty system in Denmark means that the balance of political power changes little from one election to another. Many governments have been coalitions—agreements among the various parties to govern jointly. Thus each government will include members of parliament from a number of political parties. The result of the 1981 general election, for example, elected members of parliament representing 13 different parties.

10

Education in Denmark

Some Danish children attend pre-school classes when they are six but all children in Denmark go to school between the ages of seven and sixteen. The school day begins at eight o'clock and, after a lunch break at noon, there are lessons until two o'clock when the younger children go home, although older pupils stay on for more lessons.

Danish pupils have holidays at Easter, during the summer, in October, and at Christmas; and, additionally, an extra day's holiday during some months.

Many pupils transfer to a high school when they are 15 or 16, study for examinations, and then possibly go on to a university (at Copenhagen, Aarhus, Aalborg, Odense, or Roskilde) at about the age of 18. Those pupils who pass the Student Examination at the end of their school careers are then able to wear a white student cap with red band and black peak and may proceed, if they wish, to one of the universities to study for a degree. Others go to a technical college or academy. Some go to the Technical

University in Copenhagen, founded in 1829, which maintains high standards in engineering skills.

Denmark has a rather unusual institution in the folk high school. This is a kind of college often situated in the countryside and adults, from 18 to 80, are welcome to join. The aim of these schools is to provide a general education for adults. Such subjects as Danish, Danish history, world history, literature, politics, religion, and psychology are all taught. There are no examinations at these folk high schools. The first folk high school was opened in the middle of the 19th century and one of the pioneers in this field was Bishop Grundtvig. There is a church with an unusual stepped design in its facade named after him on Bishop's Hill in Copenhagen. The church was completed in 1940 and is built of yellow bricks.

The languages of Denmark, Sweden, and Norway are closely related. Scholars believe that they may have arisen from a common language spoken throughout Scandinavia more than a thou-

69

sand years ago. Danes are able to communicate fairly easily with Norwegians but not quite so easily with Swedes.

Pupils at Danish schools must learn to speak English from about the age of 12. Some also learn German or French and become tri-lingual.

Here are a few words of Danish from which you will see that it is not exactly easy for an English-speaker to understand!

rødgrød med fløde	fruit and jelly with cream
smørrebrød	open sandwich
skraekkelig	frightful
ødelaegge	spoil
spørgsmål	question
ø	island

Other words are rather easier for an English-speaker to understand since they are similar to English:

fader	father
hus	house
komme	come
liv	life
mand	man
aeg	egg

The Danish alphabet has extra letters: ø (which sounds like the *u* in "fur"), *ae* joined together (which sounds like the *e* in "get"), and *å*—sometimes written *aa*—(which sounds like the *aw* in "paw").

There are many dialects in Denmark. For example, the dialect of Jutland differs greatly from the "standard Danish" spoken in and around Copenhagen. The people on the island of Bornholm sound more like Swedes than Danes.

The Danes are a literate people with a high standard of education. Over 50 newspapers are published throughout the country. Two important daily newspapers are the *Berlingske Tidende* (a Conservative paper) and the *Politiken* (a Social-Liberal paper). The Danes publish an impressive number of books each year and many millions of books are borrowed from the libraries throughout the country.

Bishop Grundtvig's church in Copenhagen—note the unusual stepped design in its facade.

11

Danish Traditions

The Danes regularly fly their red flag with its white cross. Many Danish families have a flagpole in their garden, smaller flags to hold in the hand on festive occasions, and even tiny ones to fix in lapels. Small flags are stuck on children's birthday cakes and strings of paper flags are hung on Christmas trees. A Danish citizen has the right to fly the flag of Denmark where and when he likes, and most do so at the slightest excuse. They are proud of their flag and of their heritage. Following are some of their customs and traditions.

Some Danes still wear traditional wooden shoes since these clogs last for a long time and are comfortable, especially for people whose occupations entail standing for any length of time—people such as nurses, shop-assistants, and housewives.

In the time of Hans Christian Andersen when many more people wore clogs, Denmark was the land of storks. There are fewer today. Even so, at Ribe, near Esbjerg on the Jutland peninsula, the inhabitants have become used to these huge birds building their nests on chimneys or roofs. They appear in Denmark in the spring after spending the winter in Africa. But the marshlands (where they once found frogs to eat) are shrinking, as land is reclaimed for farming. The people of Ribe still fix landing places such as cartwheels on their roofs, in the hope that storks will nest on the house. The nest is regarded as a sign of good luck.

In Denmark, bonfires are lit on the eve of midsummer, just as they were in ancient times, to celebrate the arrival of the longest day of the year. A witch with a broomstick is hoisted on the fire and burned to symbolize the destruction of evil. This is supposed to send the witches out of the country on their broomsticks. They fly off to a mountain in the north of Germany leaving Denmark safe for another year!

A visitor who has been invited to a Danish home would be well-advised to arrive on time; being late is frowned upon. There is much handshaking on arrival. The Danes shake hands very often and with enthusiasm. The word *tak* (meaning "thank you") is also used very commonly.

Toasting someone's health with a raised glass is a complicated Scandinavian ritual. The word to use is *skål* but the process is complex; glasses must be lifted and glances exchanged in a particular way.

The Danes love flowers and grow them not only in their gardens but also indoors; house plants often have pride of place on windowsills. It is usual for a guest to take flowers to the hostess, especially when he visits for the first time.

There is a fairly limited number of different surnames in

Denmark due to a law in the early 19th century which made each family choose one surname. (Prior to that time, a boy or girl added *sen* [son] or *datter* [daughter] to their father's Christian name. A man called Erik Ejlers might have had a son called Jens Eriksen and a daughter called Ella Erikdatter. This was very confusing and the law of 1828 aimed at simplifying the system.) But there are now so many Hansens, Petersens, Larsens, Jensens, Nielsens, and so on, in Denmark that any one surname is listed in the telephone directory according to occupation!

Another custom is that it is usual to address someone (either verbally or on an envelope) by giving them their full title: Mr. Civil Engineer Niels Petersen.

Danish schoolchildren are given a holiday from school on the Queen's birthday. Another popular day with children is the Monday before Shrove Tuesday when some children wear fancy dress and go around collecting cakes and sweets—much as children in Britain collect coins for Guy Fawkes day in November, and children in the United States go "trick or treating" at Halloween.

Another popular tradition in Denmark is the use of candles. They are used as decorations in many homes. There are candles made in a wide variety of colors and in attractive shapes. In May each year, on Liberation Day, some Danes place lighted candles in their windows to remember the glad day at the end of the Second World War, when Denmark ceased to be an occupied country.

Traditional dress is seldom worn in Denmark, except on a few islands such as Fanø (near Esbjerg). Even there, such costumes

74

Children celebrating Fanø Day, a local holiday on the island of Fanø. This is one of the few places in Denmark where traditional dress is still worn on special occasions.

only appear on special festival days. Folkdance groups make traditional costumes for performances and festivals. The national dress for women consists of full-skirted dresses with long sleeves, attractive aprons, embroidered bonnets, and perhaps clogs. Men wear tunic coats, trousers that are tucked into high leather boots, and perhaps a hat or woollen cap.

A Danish chimney sweep still dresses in old-fashioned clothes, including a tall, black silk hat, while climbing about on roofs doing his job. In Denmark, a chimney sweep cleans the chimney

A folk-dance group in national costume.

of an open fire by dropping a long brush down it. He does not push a brush up the chimney from inside the house.

One old custom that is still observed in many parts of the country is that of hanging large model ships inside churches, suspended from the roof. Perhaps this is not so surprising in the light of the importance of ships and the sea to this mainly island people.

The beech is the national tree of Denmark. There are beech woods in many parts of the countryside. When the beech leaves unfurl in the spring, this is a welcome signal for the Danes to take

76

trips into the countryside to walk in the woods and enjoy the fresh green colors of the trees now that winter has ended.

The cold and dark of winter is, of course, relieved by Christmas when it is traditional in Denmark to eat goose, duck, or roast pork. Some families also eat rice pudding at the start of the Christmas dinner and hope that their portion will contain a hidden almond, for this brings a gift to the finder.

Parents try to decorate the tree secretly on Christmas Eve. Many families go to church in the early evening and the Christmas meal follows. The candles on the tree are then lit and the children are allowed to see the tree for the first time. The family walk around the tree singing carols. A few presents are opened, then there are more carols, then more presents. Christmas Eve in Denmark is more important than Christmas Day which follows.

The Danes are very interested in the lifestyles of their ances-

A brightly-decorated Christmas tree in the center of Copenhagen.

tors. There are many museums and reconstructed buildings in Denmark. And large numbers of old buildings in towns and villages are cared for and lived in by their owners who have a possessive pride in both the past and the present. That is why the old and the new, the traditional and the experimental, are able to exist comfortably side by side in so many aspects of life in Denmark.

At Lejre, in the center of Zealand, for example, there is an unusual reconstruction of an Iron-Age settlement where archaeologists have built Iron-Age huts and experimented with early farming methods. The open-air museum also has reconstructions of buildings from more recent centuries, and Danish school children visit the center in groups to assist with the experiments and to learn how the people of Denmark lived and worked in the past.

The reconstruction of an Iron-Age settlement at Lejre, in the center of Zealand—where Danes can see for themselves how their ancestors lived and worked.

12

Famous Danes

Denmark and its citizens are not often in the headlines of the world news. But throughout history there have been Danes who made their mark—either as scholars or in fields of practical achievement. We have space to mention only a few of them.

Tycho Brahe was a 16th-century astronomer who was given the island of Hven in the Sound on which to work. He built observatories there and produced the world's first reliable catalog of the stars.

Ole Römer was another famous Danish scientist (1644-1710). He calculated the speed of light and also constructed a thermometer with a scale based on the freezing and boiling points of water.

In the fields of religion and education, the most renowned name is that of Bishop Grundtvig who wrote nearly 1,500 hymns and songs and who helped to found Denmark's folk high schools.

Another Dane, Knud Rasmussen, lived among the Eskimos early in the 20th century making many expeditions to different parts of Greenland. He traveled from Greenland to Bering Strait in the period 1921-1924 during which time he visited and studied most of the various Eskimo tribes.

Also in the 20th century, a Dane named Niels Bohr was one of the founders of modern atomic theory and nuclear research. This was a period when science and industry worked hand in hand. For example, Mads Clausen began the Danfoss Company which made specialized equipment, such as refrigerator and central heating components, which were sold to more than 100 countries. Hans Wegner designed attractive and functional modern furniture that gave new life to furniture design not only in Denmark but throughout the world. And Karl Krøyer invented synopal, a material for road surfaces, which seems to be virtually white from a distance and thus greatly improves visibility for motorists, reducing the frequency of accidents.

The most well-known Dane of all was a writer of folk tales and fairy stories. Hans Christian Andersen was born in 1805 in the city of Odense, on Funen, into a poor family. His father was a cobbler and his mother a washerwoman. He was the only child in the family and he lived for much of his childhood in a dream world. His father died when Hans was 11 years old. The boy spent his time making puppets and toy theaters and reading as many books as he was able to borrow. At first, he hoped to be an opera singer. When he was 14 he left home and went to Copenhagen. Life in the bustling capital must have seemed strange and exciting to this boy from the island of Funen. At that time Copenhagen was a walled city. At night the gates in the wall were locked, and the keys were kept by the king until morning. It

A statue of the writer Hans Christian Andersen, possibly the most famous Dane of all.

was rumored that the king slept with the keys of the city gates under his pillow.

Despite having auditions, the boy was unsuccessful as a singer. It was then that he decided to become a writer. He was sent to school and then to university. He won a scholarship and, using this money, he traveled and wrote about his wanderings. His first book of fairy tales was published in 1835 and he became world-famous as a writer.

Hans Christian Andersen was a little like the ugly duckling (in one of his most famous stories) that grew into a swan. He sought inspiration for his stories from the people and places around him and most of his tales have Danish settings. Andersen was at Gisselfeld Castle when he had the idea for *The Ugly Duckling*. The castle with its moat, dock leaves, storks, wild swans and, of course, ducks, provided the inspiration for one of the most famous stories in the world:

> *Bathed in sunshine stood an old manor house with a deep moat round it, and growing out of the wall down by the water were huge dock leaves... The place was as tangled and twisty as the densest forest, and here it was that a duck was sitting on her nest.*

Similarly, most of the characters in his stories were typical Danes—people such as peasants, farmers' wives, soldiers, students, kings, queens, princes, and princesses. He not only used

Gisselfeld Castle, which provided the inspiration for one of Hans Christian Andersen's best-loved stories, *The Ugly Duckling*.

the people and places of his acquaintance as characters and settings for his tales but incorporated details of landscape and climate to make the stories spring to life as in the *Snow Man* when he wrote:

> *All the trees and bushes were covered with hoar-frost; it was like a whole forest of white coral. . . everything sparkled as if it had been sprinkled over with diamond dust.*

His tales have been translated into more than 100 different languages—including Japanese and Chinese. His stories became popular—as they still are today—because the reader could see in them pictures not only of Denmark but of far-off places too. He wrote at times about sad events because he knew that unhappiness may come to anyone. But also that goodness and honest love can be used to break the spell of evil thoughts and to combat meanness and sadness.

Andersen must have been a strange sight—a tall, thin man with a long nose, wearing a top hat and black coat, and carrying a walking-stick. Some thought him ugly. When he traveled and stayed in hotels he carried in his luggage a long rope which he could use if he ever needed to escape through the window in case of fire. His was indeed a "rags to riches" story. He once wrote that he had arrived in Copenhagen carrying a little parcel as a poor, unknown youth but that fortune had smiled on him and he became so well-known that he had been invited to visit the queen.

He lived in rented rooms on the waterfront at Copenhagen. He

Hans Christian Andersen's traveling equipment, including the rope which he carried with him in case fire broke out and he was forced to escape through a window.

never married and when he died in 1875, at the age of 70, he was a lonely man. His gravestone in a Copenhagen cemetery bears a simple inscription meaning "The Poet."

13

Living in Denmark

Homes in Denmark vary from modern, functional apartments, to large and rather grand houses dating from the 17th, 18th, or 19th century, to well-designed bungalows. The bungalows are planned by architects to include picture windows, attractive fireplaces, parquet flooring, and simple but attractive design.

Bedrooms in the newer houses tend to be rather small but the living space is made as large as possible. This may be an open-plan living area without doors to separate the various sections of space. Bathrooms are sometimes very small and some of them contain a bathtub. This has a shallow end where you sit and a deeper end where you place your feet.

Most homes have central heating and double glazing to help combat the cold of winter. Many have steep roofs which allow rooms to be built in the roof space.

The detached house built for a single family and standing in its own garden now faces competition from low-rise, terraced, and cluster housing of two or three stories. Some of the housing estates built on the outskirts of Copenhagen are located among trees in an attempt to preserve the natural beauty of the countryside. About 60 percent of the housing in Denmark is owner-occupied. The remainder of the houses are rented dwellings, often in multi-story blocks.

There are several thousand sports clubs in Denmark and many Danes take part in sports of one kind or another. Swimming, canoeing, cycling, boxing, boating, soccer, golf, riding, tennis, athletics, badminton, and fishing for trout, pike, and carp are all popular. Most of the Danes who indulge in sports do so for the pleasure of the game, to meet friends or to enjoy the fresh air. In Denmark sports are mainly for recreation and relaxation rather than being played in a competitive spirit of going all out to win.

Christianity has existed in Denmark for almost a thousand years. In the 13th century there was a revival of interest in religion in Denmark. About 800 village churches dating from the medieval period are a reminder of this religious enthusiasm. During the reign of King Christian III (1534-1539) at the time of the Reformation, the Lutheran religion was introduced into Denmark and the first Bible in Danish was printed.

Almost everyone in Denmark belongs to the national Lutheran Church, although only a small percentage of Danes attend church regularly. Most Danes pay an annual church tax in order to help support the work of the large number of churches throughout the country.

Other Danes belong to the Methodist, Baptist and Roman Catholic churches. There is also a small Jewish community.

The monetary unit is the Danish *krone* (crown) and this is abbreviated to *Dkr* to distinguish it from the krone of Sweden and Norway. One krone is worth 100 øre. There are banknotes in circulation for 1,000, 500, 100, 50, and 20 kroner. There are coins valued at 10, 5, and one krone; and 25, 10, and 5 øre. The 25 øre coin has a hole in the center to distinguish it from the one krone coin which is about the same size.

In summer, many Danes visit the coast and enjoy the sandy beaches and the sea-bathing. Others spend part of their vacation on a farm, especially if their usual home is in a town. On the other hand, families from the country may have their vacation in one of the towns or cities.

In the 19th century, town-dwellers who could afford to do so used to spend seaside vacations staying at the houses of people who had rooms to rent for the summer. Some town-dwellers then began to build their own cottages by the sea for weekends and vacations. Most of these cottages were little more than simple cabins suitable only for summer occupation. Now, however, many have been vastly improved to form comfortable, well-insulated, and fully-equipped dwellings that can be used at any time of the year. Their function has changed from that of summer cottage to second home. Many families fortunate enough to have such a second home simply spend part of the year in one and the remainder of the year in the other, without any loss of modern conveniences or comfort when they move.

Most Danes are now town-dwellers and whenever they can they take trips into the countryside to enjoy the beauty of the woods, the fields, and the fresh air. A large number of families own one of these second properties, perhaps a tiny chalet or wooden bungalow built in a clearing a short distance from a town, or perhaps a larger, grander house. But, whatever its size, it is always likely to have a small garden and a flagpole from which the family proudly flies its Danish flag when in residence. The yard may be just about big enough for a few deck chairs and a small table for outdoor snack meals. The Danes love to visit these second homes in the country where they can relax during weekends and vacations. Children from towns and cities find much to explore and enjoy in the different environment of rural Denmark.

Those who cannot afford a second home may rent an allotment garden just outside the town to grow flowers and vegetables. There will probably be a shed on the allotment large enough to take a couple of bunk beds and a camping stove so that the family can perhaps stay for a night or two. Inevitably, there will be a flag to hoist, although this is always taken down before sunset.

The Danes are very interested in their food. Food shops and cafés tempt passersby with attractively laid out cold dishes in the windows. Seafood forms an important part of the national menu.

The Danes tend to eat little but often during a typical day, and their food is prepared to a high standard.

88

Breakfast usually consists of various kinds of bread, with butter, and cheese or jam. Coffee, tea, and milk are popular drinks. At lunchtime many Danes eat an open sandwich—a slice of rye bread on which may be piled such tempting delicacies as meat, cheese, fish, egg, ham, salad, or vegetables. The tasty juices sink down to the bread base and improve the flavor of the bread. The Danish word for an open sandwich is *smørrebrød* (literally meaning "buttered bread"). Lager is almost the national drink of Denmark

An interior by the designer Johannes Hansen. The Danes have acquired a worldwide reputation for well-designed homes and furnishings in a simple, uncluttered style.

and a glass of lager or beer is often part of this lunchtime snack. Some people eat pastries and cream cakes in the afternoon. The main meal of the day is eaten in the early evening. There may also be a snack late at night.

There are a number of national dishes. Asparagus, grown on Danish farms, is served with butter in the early summer. Herring, cured on the island of Bornholm, is a speciality. Fish is greatly enjoyed. A favorite is plaice served with butter, parsley and new potatoes. Minced fish or meat are often eaten. Young lobsters are a delicacy and boiled cod is served with mustard sauce and melted butter. Eels are fried in butter. "Beer-bread" is another Danish speciality: it is rye bread boiled in water to which beer, lemon, sugar, and milk are added to make a sort of thick soup. Beer is

90

also added to pancakes. The most popular dessert in the summer is strawberries and cream. Danish blue (which is white with blue veins), Havarti (light yellow with holes that appear during the maturing process), Samsøe (mild and nourishing and eaten by many Danes virtually every day), Brie, and Camembert are all popular cheeses. Fruits, vegetables, and nuts are often served with cheeses on open sandwiches.

Typical drinks are Carlsberg and Tuborg beer and lager. Cherry heering (a cherry brandy which is the national liqueur of Denmark) and blackcurrant rum are popular liqueurs. Cherry orchards in Denmark provide the vast number of cherries that are needed to make the cherry brandy. *Schnapps* (sometimes called *akvavit*) is a strong white spirit often drunk in Denmark. It is gulped down from small glasses and followed by sips of beer.

14

The Economy

Denmark has no coalfields, hydroelectric power, minerals, or extensive forests. The natural resources of the country are the soil and the initiative of the people in creating an efficient economy. This lack of raw materials, coupled with a well-placed geographical position (between the other Scandinavian countries and the rest of Europe) has helped to make Denmark into a trading nation. Traditionally, the economy of Denmark has depended on the export of agricultural produce in order to maintain a high standard of living. Exported food products include butter, ham, bacon, condensed milk, and beet sugar. Danish dairy products are exported to about 125 countries—the majority of countries in the world.

Denmark depends greatly on two foreign markets, Britain and Germany, where it sells many of its exports. These two countries receive about 30 percent of Denmark's total exports; other countries of the European Union receive about 20 percent. Norway,

Sweden, and the United States are other countries to which Denmark exports large quantities of farm produce and manufactured goods.

Although farming is still of vital importance to Denmark the country has developed its industries at a fast pace in recent years. Many more people are now employed in the various industries than in farming. Denmark brews lager and beer and much of this is exported. The production of glass, cement, agricultural machinery, silverware, pottery and chinaware, furniture, ships, diesel engines, and electrical equipment for dairies are all important industries.

Denmark's chief exports are industrial products. They form about 61 percent of the total. Now they are followed, a long way behind, by agricultural products (about 20 percent). It can be claimed with much truth that Denmark is no longer an agricultural country. Rather, it is an increasingly important industrial nation. The largest single group of workers in the country is employed by the iron and steel industries. Machinery is an important industrial export. Diesel engines from Denmark are exported to many countries; and the very first diesel-engine ship came from a Danish shipyard.

The Danish tourist industry is being developed and the money spent by foreign tourists in Denmark counts as an important although "invisible" export. One attraction is Legoland Park in Billund in central Jutland which is popular with visitors from abroad. It contains many unusual and intricate models made from

Lego bricks, among which visitors stroll in the open-air looking like giants in a miniature world.

Denmark's main imports are raw materials for industry, as well as energy and fuel; much of these comes from Germany, Sweden, the United States, and Norway. A large number of Danes are employed in public services and in administering the country (about 30 percent); others are engaged in manufacturing industries and mining (about 19 percent); private services (about 40 percent); agriculture (about five percent); and building and construction (about six percent).

Denmark is unusual in Europe in that the industrial sector of

A model of the royal residence, Amalienborg Palace, in Legoland Park. It took 900,000 Lego bricks and 400,000 windows to build it.

the economy is in private hands. Many industrial companies in Denmark are fairly small concerns.

Ownership of the different parts of the North Sea was divided in the 1960s between the countries bordering it. Denmark received a section of the central area. In 1972, Denmark began to extract oil from the Dan Field. Several other oilfields in the Danish sector of the North Sea have since been opened up. The annual Danish oil production now serves about 20 percent of the energy needs of Denmark. This has been an important development for the country, since previously it produced no energy of its own. The oil is led through a pipeline from the North Sea across Jutland to a refinery at Fredericia.

In the 1970s the Danish Underground Consortium discovered not only oil in the North Sea but also large gas fields. The natural gas is led ashore through a pipeline on the west coast of Jutland and then distributed throughout the country (through Funen and Zealand) by a network of other pipelines. Regional companies then supply it to consumers. This Danish gas system is even connected to Germany and Sweden.

In recent years electrical power plants in Denmark have reverted to using coal as a main fuel since this is cheaper than oil. But coal prices have now risen and, in addition, Denmark is dependent on stocks obtained from abroad. Tests are being made in an attempt to provide more energy from the sun (solar heat from collectors on roofs of buildings, for instance, provides consumers with hot water during the summer months) and from the wind. Denmark is a windy country and it has been estimated that ten percent of the country's electrical power can be obtained by building windmills—including large wind turbines which are particularly useful as producers of energy. Denmark has been a member of the United Nations since its foundation in 1945. In 1949 Denmark joined NATO—the North Atlantic Treaty Organization. Like the other Scandinavian countries, Denmark is also a member of the Nordic Council.

In 1973 Denmark joined the European Economic Community (EEC), now called the European Community (EC) and part of the European Union (EU). The three most important elements of EEC cooperation are the common economic policy, free trade in industrial goods, and common financing of the activities. When Denmark joined the EEC this earned for the country higher prices for farm exports and better terms of trade.

15

Greenland and the Faroe Islands

The kingdom of Denmark includes Greenland and the Faroe Islands.

Greenland is the world's largest island. Much of it is covered with an inland ice-sheet, but there are ice-free areas along the

The harbor at Jakobshavn in western Greenland—note the ice floes in the water.

An Eskimo fisherman proudly displaying the salmon he has just caught. Salmon is regarded as a great delicacy in Denmark.

coast. Greenland has 56,500 inhabitants and these include about 10,000 Danes. The island achieved partial self-government in 1979 and has had the status of a Danish county since 1953.

Greenland is rich in minerals but it will be some time before these can be more usefully exploited. Greenlanders fish from motorized fishing vessels and modern trawlers. They export salmon, cod, shrimps, and halibut. But the traditional life of the Eskimo hunter and sealer in the north and east of Greenland has remained largely unchanged.

Greenland is not self-supporting economically and receives huge annual grants from Denmark. There are now hospitals, schools, housing developments, power stations, roads, harbors, and factories provided by Denmark.

The Faroe Islands form a self-governing community under the Danish crown. They comprise a group of 18 islands in the North Atlantic where 45,000 people live. A small percentage of the land is cultivated and much of the remainder is used as pasture for sheep. The closest neighbors of the Faroes are people on the Shetland Islands, off the north coast of Scotland. The fishing industry is the main source of income on the Faroe Islands. The people speak Faroese and they are taught in this language at school, although the children learn Danish as a second language.

16

Denmark in the Modern World

The story of Denmark is a story of success. The country is now one of the wealthiest nations in the world with a high average income per head of household. During the 20th century Denmark has become one of the most efficient and prosperous agricultural nations of the world. The agricultural sector of the economy remains important today; but, additionally, Denmark is now a predominant industrial force in the markets of the world. Rapid industrial expansion from the 1950s has resulted in industry now dominating the economy of the country in terms of exports, output, employment and the value of the country's total production. The Danes (80 percent of them now live in towns and cities) have become masters of the art of importing raw materials, processing them in their factories, and then exporting the finished products. Shipbuilding, for instance, is one such important heavy industry in Denmark that is dependent on imported raw materials.

The Danish firm of construction engineers that built a bridge over the Gudenaa (Denmark's only river) in the early 20th century went on to build bridges in Germany, Britain, and other countries in all parts of the world. The success story of this one firm has been repeated many times in all sectors of Danish industrial development.

A highway section of a bridge was partially completed in 1998 across the Great Belt, joining Zealand and Funen. This bridge was a longtime in planning and took over 10 years to build, and when fully completed will be an intricate network of bridges and tunnels. At 12 miles (19 kilometers) long, it is one of the longest bridges in the world. A bridge may also be built across the Sound, so linking Sweden with Denmark.

The words of a Danish poem tell the story of Denmark:

Path of the Dane to fame and might!
Dark rolling wave!

The people in this land of islands, practically surrounded by sea, have had the capacity and enterprise to adapt themselves again and again to the needs of a changing world economy. The Danes are hard-working, cheerful, and optimistic; and the Danish word *hygge* (meaning "to make oneself comfortable") describes their way of life at home where they like to surround themselves with useful and attractive possessions. They live in a pleasant land and even the Danish national anthem speaks of the "lovely land with its broad beaches." Bishop Grundtvig's ideal for Denmark expressed in the 19th century that the country should be a land where "few have too much and fewer too little" seems to be fast approaching.

GLOSSARY

archipelago   A group of islands in a large body of water

berth   The act of placing a ship at rest by dropping an anchor

coniferous   An evergreen tree bearing cones, such as the pine and cypress trees

danegold   Danish word for ransom

danneborg   The Danish word for their flag, it means a piece of red cloth

dike   A bank of dirt or a wall constructed to control or confine water

estuary   A water passage where the tide meets a river current; especially an arm of the sea at the lower end of a river

fiord   Long narrow arm of the sea, commonly extending far inland

lager   A light beer matured in refrigeration

North Atlantic Drift   A warm current in the north Atlantic Ocean that raises the winter temperatures in Denmark due to wind blowing over the warm water

peat-bog	Type of wetland characterized by wet, spongy, poorly drained peaty soil
prow	Front of a ship or boat
quay	A dock
runic characters	Script of the ancient north Germanic tribes
Shrove Tuesday	The day before Ash Wednesday and the beginning of the Christian season of Lent. It is usually a day of celebration.
trawler	One who fishes by dragging a large net along the bottom of the sea to gather fish or marine life
turrets	A small tower usually an ornamental structure at an angle from a larger structure
wattle and daub	A method of constructing walls in which wooden stakes (wattles) are woven with horizontal twigs and branches and then daubed with clay or mud

INDEX

A

Aalborg, 53
Aarhus (Arhus), 51-52
Absalom, Bishop, 9, 34, 43
Aero, 19
Air travel, 42
Agriculture, 19, 20-21, 23, 55-60
Alfred the Great, 32
Alphabet (Danish), 70
Amagar, 49
Amalienborg Palace, 44
Amber, 24
Andersen, Hans Christian, 52, 80-84
Archaelogy, 22-23, 24, 25, 26

B

Baltic Sea, 13, 14, 19, 23, 35, 63
Beech trees, 76-77
Bicycles, 42
Bohr, Niels, 80
Bone Age, 23
Bonfires, 73
Bornholm, 19, 63
Brahe, Tycho, 79
Bridges, 101

Britain, 9, 10, 23, 28, 29, 30-31, 32-33, 36,-37, 39, 64
Bromme, 22

C

Canute, 32, 33
Cattle, 20
Cheese, 57, 91
Chimney-sweep, 75
Christian III, 86
Christian IV, 43
Christian X, 38
Christiansborg Palace, 43, 65
Christianity, Christians, 9, 33, 86-87
Christmas, 77
Clausen, Mads, 80
Climate, 13-14
Clothing, 24
Cooperative societies, 56-57
Copenhagen, 9, 18, 36, 38, 41, 43-50
Costumes (traditional), 72, 74-75
Crops, 19, 20, 21, 55, 57-59
Crown Jewels, 45
Currency, 87

D

Dairies, 55, 57
Dairy produce, 55, 57, 92
Danegold, 33
Dannebrag. *See* flag

E

Economy, 56, 92-96
Education, 68-71
Elsinore, 13, 35
England. *See* Britain
Eriksen, Edvard, 48
Esbjerg, 41, 54, 62
Estonians, 33
Europe, 18, 28
European Economic Community, 11, 96
European Union, 11-12, 96
Exports, 63, 92, 93

F

Falster, 18, 23, 40
Fanø, 74
Farms, farming. *See* agriculture
Faroe Islands, 97, 99
Finland, 13
Fiords, 17
First World War, 10, 37
Fishing, 61-64
Flag, 34, 72
Flowers, 73
Folk high school, 69
Food, 88-91
Forests, 59
France, French, 28, 29
Frederick IV, 10, 35
Frederick VII, 65

Frederick IX, 11
Frederikshavn, 62
Funen, 13, 14, 19, 23, 41, 52

G

Gasfields, 95
Geography, 14-16, 21
Germans, Germany, 11, 13, 20, 37, 38
Gold, 27
Gorm the Old, 32
Government, 65-67
Granite, 19
Great Belt, 14, 41, 42
Great Stream Bridge, 40
Greenland, 97-99
Grundtvig, Bishop, 69, 79, 101
Gudenaa River, 14

H

Harald Bluetooth, 9, 27, 32
Herring, 63
Holidays, 74
Houses, 23, 85-86
Hydrofoil service, 40

I

Ice ages, 15
Imports, 94
Industries, 50, 61, 93-95
Islands, 18-21

J

Jelling Stone, 32
Jutland, 13, 15, 18, 19-20, 23, 41, 51, 53, 54, 58, 62

K

Kattegat, 63
Korsør, 41
Kronborg Castle, 35, 36
Krøyer, Karl, 80

L

Langeland, 19
Languages, 69-71
League of Armed Neutrality, 36
League of Nations, 10
Legoland Park (Billund), 93
Lejre, 78
Liberation Day, 74
Little Mermaid, The, 48
Lolland, 18, 23, 41
Lutheranism, 10, 86

M

Maastricht Treaty, 11
Margrethe I (Queen), 9, 34
Margrethe II (Queen), 11, 65
Market gardens, 58-59
Mink farms, 59
Møn, 16, 18

N

Napoleonic Wars, 10, 35-36, 43
National Day, 65
National Museum (Copenhagen), 24, 45
NATO, 11
Natural resources, 95
Nelson, Admiral Lord, 36
North Atlantic Drift, 14
North Sea, 13, 21, 23, 30, 63, 95

Norway, Norwegians, 13, 28, 32, 35, 37

O

Occupation (German), 38-39
Occupations (work), 94
Odense, 52, 80
Oil, 95

P

Parliament, 66, 67
Pigs, 20, 55, 57
Political parties, 67
Population, 13, 20, 48

R

Rådhus (City Hall), 45
Railways, 41, 42
Randers, 54
Rasmussen, Knud, 79-80
Rasmussen, Prime Minister, 12
Religion, 33, 86-87
Resistance fighters, 39
Ribe, 72
Romans, 26
Römer, Ole, 79
Rosenborg Palace, 43, 45
Roskilde, 43
Runes, 32
Russia, 36

S

Scheswig-Holstein, 10, 37
Schnapps, 53, 91
Second World War, 38, 39
Silkeborg Museum, 26
Skagerrak, 62

Sound Dues (taxes), 35
Sports, 86
Stone Age, New, 23
Storks, 72
Surnames, 73-74
Sweden, Swedes, 10, 13, 18, 27, 28,
    32, 35, 36, 37

T
Taasinge, 19
Thorvaldsen, Bertel, 46
Tivoli gardens, 46-47
Tollund Man, 11, 25, 26
Tourism, 93-94
Traditions, 73-77
Transportation, 40-42

Treaty of Versailles, 10, 37
Trelleborg, 31-32

V
Vacations, 87-88
Valdemar the Great, 34
Viking ships, 30
Vikings, 9, 28-30

W
Wegner, Hans, 80
Wends, 34

Z
Zealand, 13, 14, 18-19, 22, 23, 40,
    41, 49, 78